COASTAL GARDENING: WITH

Coastal Gardening

WITH TREES AND SHRUBS

Eric Leah

Photographs by the Author
Illustrations by Jenny Weaver

ABERCASTLE PUBLICATIONS

Front Cover Photograph:
Laburnum, Rhododendrons and Sitka Spruce windbreak

Back Cover:
The author working in his Polytunnel, showing Morning Glory (Ipomoea) at doorway

Contents

CHAPTER 1

Can I Make a Garden Here?

"My house is on a cliff edge with the full blast of winds coming in from the sea, where even the nettles are burned black! Is there any chance of growing anything?" This is obviously the worst site, but a garden of a kind is possible. What kind, largely depends on 1. How much time and money you want to spend on the garden. 2. How ambitious you want to be. 3. Whether or not you will erect some kind of wind barrier.

This third point is linked with the question of preserving one's view, and this depends on a. view from the house, b. view standing, or c. view sitting in the garden. If a wind barrier was erected, it could be six feet high, if one only demanded a view from the house, but five feet high if viewed standing in the garden, but only three and a half feet high if one must preserve the sea view from a garden seat. Should your choice be the latter, then some kind of the 'low profile' garden is the only possible kind.

A 'low profile' garden is one composed mainly of low and dwarf shrubs, alpines herbs, dwarf and prostrate conifers and heathers. Most of the plants should be in the 6-12 inch range, with occasional plants at 2-3 feet (ultimate size). If there is no wind barrier at all, then the choice and variety of plants is very small, and would probably have to be prostrate junipers, heathers, sedums, thrift and mat-forming alpines such as dianthus, aubrieta, arabis, alyssum etc. Without some kind of .wind barrier (if only 2-3 feet high) growth would be exceedingly slow, and losses high.

On this worst possible site, the cliff edge type of property, the making

7

of a sunken garden would be a tremendous help. This could be as little as a ten feet diameter hollow for sunbathing or sitting in. The excavated soil can be built up around the windward side, and on the leeward side, one could grow alpines and heathers. This sunken garden must be on well drained soil or a drainage system installed.

On this worst possible site, a lawn is possible, preferably sown in April. Annual and perennial flowers, and herbs could be all grown, if planted March/April, so that they are well established before winter. Strawberries, blackcurrants and gooseberries are also possible, and some vegetables. A minimum of three feet high windbreak would help the plants to get established, a taller one preferable. However, if no windbreak is erected at all, growth will be slow, and losses from severe gales can be expected.

It is assumed that the soil is reasonably fertile and well supplied with humus if one is to grow all the crops mentioned in this paragraph. Otherwise, the soil must be supplied with bonemeal, seaweedmeal or any long lasting organic manures, plus all the farmyard manure, compost, leafmould etc., that you can get. The crops must also be fed with Growmore fertiliser between April and August.

"Under what conditions does one give up altogether?" This cannot be answered in a simple straightforward way, because it depends on several factors such as (i) is the soil poor or almost non existent? (ii) what is the age of the gardener? (iii) how much time and energy, can the gardener give? Again, assuming the worst possible situation, i.e. poor sandy or very shallow soil, a gardener who is retired and wishes to expend the minimum time and energy on his garden, then a modified 'low profile' garden and a lawn and a few herbs and other perennials are all possible. How successful he or she is in this limited garden obviously depends on both the skill and dynamic of the gardener — and the weather!

When we came to Pembrokeshire in 1951, most people considered that we were quite mad to want to start a market garden and nursery on our wet, windswept seven acres of silty clay loam. The advisors for the Ministry of Agriculture actually persuaded us to sell up, and buy another smallholding they knew of, with better soil and better situation. However, I am a very obstinate person, and we loved the situation. its nearness to the sea, and in unspoilt, peaceful countryside, and the view is fantastic! So I was determined to put up with the soil and the constant gales. But it is a constant battle, every winter brings new problems. My motto has always been "Where there's a will, there's a way." For in truth, nothing is impossible, given a little time and energy. Most gardeners, may choose an easier way, I hope that the following ten chapters will prove helpful in this connection.

Creating a garden on a hilltop, on poor wet soil, with high rainfall and lots of wind, is almost as bad a site as the seaside cliff edge property, but it has a slight advantage. The seaside site has salt winds that burn the leaves of many plants, whilst the mountain site may have lots of wind, but little or no salt. However, success will depend on the choice of plants, mainly moisture loving or moisture tolerant plants, unless a drainage scheme is installed or raised beds designed.

Gardens sited ½ mile, ¾ mile or one mile from the coast, or even as far as 3 or 4 miles inland, will all be similarly placed as to what one can grow, if they all suffer exposure to winds from off the sea. However, any of these positions could very much modify the climate, if buildings, trees, hedges or a rise in the land, gave even a degree of protection from the sea winds. In this case, a lot more is possible, see Chapter 7.

One final word for the retired person who wants a garden by the coast and a very minimum of time spent on upkeep. This too is possible, if enough time and thought is spent on the initial layout, choice of plants, preparation of ground, and planting and feeding.

Ground-cover plants are one obvious choice, or a large expanse of heathers with a few dwarf conifers in between, for contrast. Weed growth around trees and shrubs either in a lawn, or a shrubbery, could be eliminated by planting through a black polythene mulch, which is afterwards covered with small gravel (½ inch or less) to hide it.

The garden could be a patio with a pool, with three or four of the 2 x 2 feet paving slabs removed in order to accommodate a few special plants. The other plants could all be in troughs, tubs or containers. Some such scheme as this will minimise both the labour, and the upkeep on the garden.

CHAPTER 2

The Problem of Wind

SALT WINDS FROM THE SEA

In coastal gardens there is always wind, but the gales off the sea are the damaging ones. Whilst they are liable to blow up at any time, even in summer, they are at their worst in autumn and winter. For this reason it is better, in really exposed gardens, to avoid planting during the period November to end of February, or even to end of March, depending on the severity of the gales. It will be necessary to water the March-April, and later, planted shrubs and trees, but this is preferable to subjecting them to six months of gale force winds immediately after planting.

Although the plants mentioned in chapters 4-6 will grow without the necessity of a windbreak, nevertheless some kind of man made shelter will speed up growth considerably.

This artificial shelter can be of fine wire netting, plastic netting, wooden laths, wattle or chestnut fencing etc., but it must not be a solid screen, but permeable. Experiments at Rosewarne Experimental Station in Cornwall, have proved that a screen with approximately 50% permeability is most effective. In the long run this will prove a good investment and could take the place of a boundary fence, if the builders were suitably advised when a new house is built.

The effective shelter of such a windbreak for garden purposes can be measured by multiplying the height of the artificial screen by 10, and in very windy situations half the distance. Thus a garden 60 feet long in a

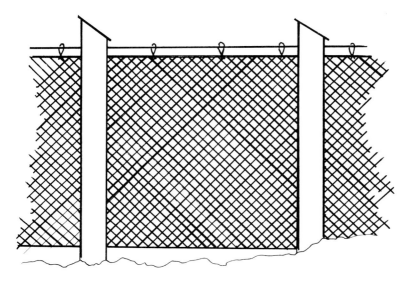

Fine mesh wire netting.

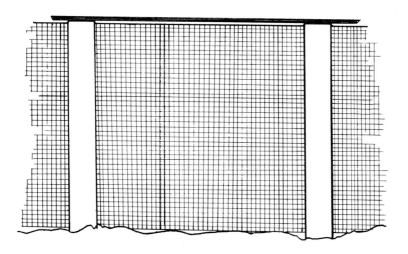

Woven plastic netting.

11

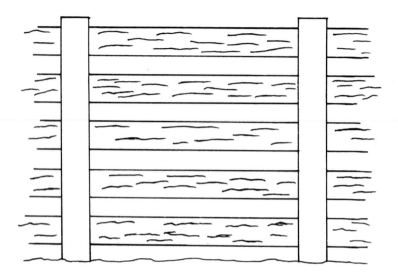

Wooden Laths.

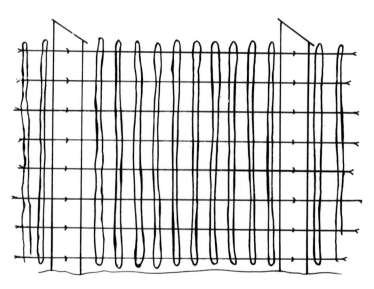

Wattle or Chestnut fencing.

moderately windy situation, could be totally protected by a 6 feet high barrier. Whilst the same garden in a very exposed situation would need a 12 feet high barrier.

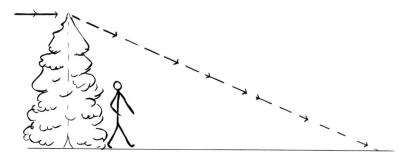

A very exposed garden. Hedge 12 feet tall. Effective shelter 60 feet.

A moderately exposed garden. Hedge 6 feet tall. Effective shelter 60 feet.

In 1951 when we took over a seven acre smallholding near the sea, we found all the hawthorn, blackthorn and gorse on the boundary banks leaning away from the wind, and severely pruned on the windward side. We are approximately one mile from the coast in N or NE direction, and approximately four miles from the coast in a W direction, and are 350-400 feet above sea level. Our land slopes to the SW, is very windswept, and ravaged by gales for at least six months in the year. Yet, by the use of Sitka Spruce, Alders, Willows and Cupressus, we have created windbreaks which enable us to grow in our nurseries a multitude of shrubs and trees from all over the world, including exotics and Mediterranean plants.

We were able to utilise the four feet high existing banks as windbreaks for the early years of growth, by planting at the foot of the bank on the leeward side. The Sitka spruce trees are now 25-28 feet high after 28 years. However, since we came here, we have planted a few Leylandii cypress, and achieved a height of 24 feet in eight years!

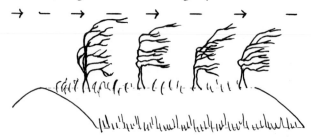

Existing banks when we arrived. Trees one sided. Growth inhibited on windward side.

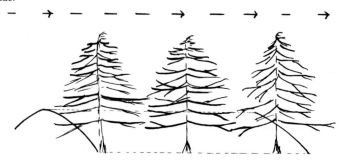

Sitka Spruce trees as a main windbreak. 28 years later.

Amongst these faster growing trees and shrubs are Pinus contorta or Beach Pine, Poplars, Willows, Alders, Ash, Larch, Leylandii cypress, Cupressus macrocarpa and Escallonia.

Gale force wind in itself is quite enough to damage or kill trees and shrubs. For apart from the obvious hazard of breaking branches, and rocking the plant until the roots break, or even blowing small plants clean out of the ground, there is another insidious factor. Constant wind, particularly gale force wind, has the effect of sucking all the moisture out of the leaves, leaving them brown as if burnt. Now, gales off the sea add one more danger to plant life, and that is the salt that is picked up from the sea, which to most plants is a killer. For remember that in times past, before the advent of modern weedicides, salt was used regularly on garden paths and drives, to kill the weeds.

After such a gale force wind from the sea, if this is followed by a dry period, it is advisable to hose down all shrubs, to wash off the salt.

FREEZING WINDS

In Britain the winter of 1977 and spring of 1978, and the very cold winter period from November 1978 to April 1979, and even more so the extreme frost of January 1982, caused more damage to trees and shrubs on our nursery (even though it is surrounded by a 20-25 feet windbreak!) than all the previous 30 years. Very low temperatures combined with northerly and easterly winds burnt shrubs and conifers, that had grown unscathed for twelve years. The early springtime was a particularly damaging period, with cold north winds that desiccated the evergreens.

When the prevailing wind is SW, a gale force wind from this direction can uproot shrubs and blow down large trees. However, the winds that cause the greatest damage and are the most difficult to screen against, are the N and E winds. These north winds are cold dry winds and they suck all the moisture out of leaves, and if it is combined with a long rainless period, young plants cannot maintain the moisture in the leaves and therefore die.

A combination of cold winds (N or E) and drought, occurred in Spring 1984, when we had six weeks of hot, dry, sunny weather. For recently planted evergreens, and particularly so with conifers, six weeks dry weather is a bleak and almost hopeless prospect, and with cold winds as well, can prove fatal to most plants. It would seem that one is on the horns of a dilemma, since springtime is the only satisfactory planting time for coastal gardens, *without protection*. Two answers remain, be patient and plant smaller plants (1-2 feet), or put up a temporary windbreak screen to protect your plants.

Rokolene netting or similar small mesh (¼ inch) netting is a very effective windbreak and is quite inexpensive. It cannot be stressed too much, that some kind of artificial barrier is absolutely essential for establishing hedges and screens in very exposed areas by the sea. Even though tough plants like Sitka spruce, pines, Eleagnus, Griselina and Escallonia are capable of withstanding sea winds on their own, without protection, they will grow and establish so much faster if they can be given some protection for the first three or four years.

15

During these periods of desiccating north winds, young plants can be helped to survive by keeping both the roots well watered and hosing the leaves twice a day with a fine spray of water. This is particularly important with conifers and evergreens.

One final point about the plant's ability to withstand both cold and wind, is the soil factor. Plants growing in a well drained soil survive severe exposure much better than those growing in wet or very heavy soil. Therefore, if you have a heavy or clay soil, then drain it or improve its texture by the addition of grit, peat and bulky humus materials dug into the surface soil.

WINDBLOWN SAND

For those who garden on sand and are very near the sea, the final problem is windblown sand, which both uproots plants and damages leaves. This must be tackled in two ways. Firstly, stabilise and enrich the poor sandy soil with humus (leaves, straw, compost, manure or peat) and secondly, to utilise ground covering plants which hug the soil, providing a living cover. Rose of Sharon — Hypericum calycinum, Periwinkles — Vinca, prostrate cotoneasters like Cotoneaster Coral Beauty, and prostrate junipers like Juniper sabina tamaricifolia, to mention only four plants, but there are a great deal more.

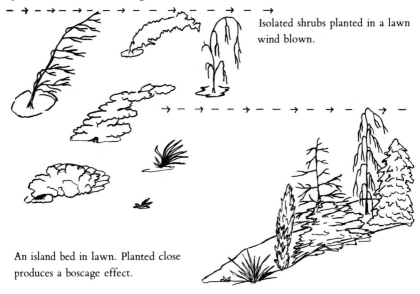

Isolated shrubs planted in a lawn wind blown.

An island bed in lawn. Planted close produces a boscage effect.

Sitka Spruce and Alders.

Cupressus macrocarpa Goldcrest, Hebe and Lavatera olbia rosea.

17

Escallonia macrantha.

Euonymus japonica.

18

Griselinia littoralis and Hippophae rhamnoides.

Pinus montana.

19

Populus alba.

Quercus ilex.

20

Sambucus aurea and escallonia.

Cordyline australis.

21

Atriplex halimus, Fuchsia and Cytisus.

Olearia.

Rosa rugosa rubra.

Tamarisk.

23

Ceanothus thyrsiflorus repens and Helianthemum.

Cistus laureofolius and Helichrysum rosmarinifolius.

24

Gardening by the sea, demands a different approach to garden planning and planting, and one golden rule is to 'plant thick'. This means planting up whole sections of the garden in one fell swoop and not a little at a time. If island beds are made in a lawn, and planted up with a mixture of suitable shrubs at a little closer distances than normal, so that in two or three years a close boscage or thicket is produced, then one plant helps another. The wind cannot uproot or blow over such plants once they have grown together, producing solid ground cover. Whereas isolated specimens dotted about at intervals, will be severely blasted by the gales.

It is far better to plant thick and to thin out at a later stage, if the trees or shrubs are growing into one another, than to plant out at the full distance apart, and leave the young plants wide open to the wind. If isolated specimens must be planted, then it may be necessary (in the winter period at any rate) to surround each one with fine netting or hessian.

THE WIND PROBLEM AND VEGETABLES

Very few vegetables can be grown satisfactorily in very exposed gardens near the sea. In a severe gale, lettuces will be bruised and burnt, runner beans and peas blown down, and young seedlings desiccated. If vegetables must be grown in such a situation, some kind of windbreak, hedge or screen of fine netting will be found most useful. This not only protects the vegetables from damaging winds, but also is instrumental in raising the temperature a few degrees on the leeward side of the netting.

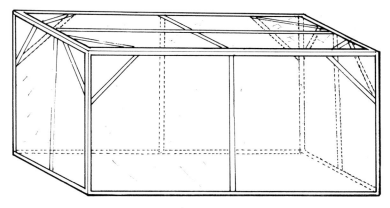

The erection of a simple wooden structure, clad with Rokelene, Netlon or Lenoweave.

25

The erection of a simple wooden structure such as is used to keep birds out of soft fruit, a 'fruit cage', made up of Netlon windbreak netting, Rokolene or Lenoweave, will make a wonderful growing area for both vegetables and fruit, in an exposed garden. It will provide conditions similar to growing in a glasshouse, without the softening effect, and high temperatures of the glass. However, it does cut down the light a little, so that crops like tomatoes, peppers and lettuce will not grow quite so well as in a glasshouse. It is infinitely better than growing them unprotected in the open.

This fine mesh plastic netting can be used streched over frames, used as cloches, made as a lean-to against a wall, or erected as a little tent around special plants, flowers or fruit. Its uses are legion, and it cannot be emphasised too much to say that by the use of such netting, growing vegetables and fruit in exposed gardens, can become a pleasure instead of a hazardous gamble.

Since wind is the major problem, it is therefore better to grow dwarf peas and beans, and all other short stemmed varieties of vegetables. In the case of runner beans, those can be grown on a strongly constructed fence of pig netting. When the plants reach the top, they are cut back, by taking a sharp sickle down the row. They now grow into a bush, and are no longer blown over, as they would be on canes.

Most vegetables will grow if the garden is provided with some kind of shelter, and since this book is primarily concerned with trees and shrubs, I shall not discuss the cultivation of the many kinds of vegetables. However, I can thoroughly recommend the growing of perpetual spinach beet, purple sprouting broccoli and leeks. These three vegetables are not only easy to grow and stand a lot of rough weather, but are very tasty and extremely valuable from a health point of view. Finally, if you want a good yield of highly flavoured vegetables, you must ensure that the soil is rich in humus and well drained, the crops grown in a sunny spot, well fed with organic fertilisers and irrigated in the summer.

CHAPTER 3

Planting, Feeding and Aftercare

TIME OF PLANTING

For coastal gardens with exposure to sea winds, we recommend spring planting. If shrubs or trees are planted at the conventional time of planting, i.e. November to March, they are subjected to five or six months of gale force winds before they can become established. Under these circumstances, many will die, and most will be so battered and burnt, that they will start growth in the spring in a very weakened state. Such plants are not likely to thrive. In our 37 years experience of gardening by the sea, we have found spring planting to be the safest and best time. There are always the odd gardens right by the coast, situated in a hollow or valley, or sheltered by banks, trees etc. Obviously, in such cases, where some protection from sea winds already exists, planting can take place in November. Everything will depend on the degree of exposure that the garden is subjected to.

PLANTING

If the shrub or tree is in a plastic container, this must be cut away before planting. *Always* plant out a *wet* soil ball, which means that if a shrub or tree in the container is dry, it must be watered before planting. In the case of large shrubs, conifers, rhododendrons etc. with a large rootball wrapped in polythene or hessian, it is best to dig the planting hole first, put in a stake if necessary, and then place the conifer, shrub etc. in the hole complete with polythene or hessian wrapping. Only when it is correctly placed in the hole, must the string be cut, and the polythene or hessian wrapping pulled from under it. It is of the utmost importance to try to retain as much soil and rootball as possible, in the case of large shrubs, conifers rhododendrons etc.

When planting, most plants will benefit from peat and bonemeal sprinkled around them in the planting hole. Give each plant two well heaped double handfuls of peat and one handful (or one ounce) of bone meal in the case of large conifers, shrubs, trees etc., less in the case of little plants such as dwarf shrubs, heathers and alpines.

STAKING

After planting, trees and tall conifers and shrubs must be securely tied to the stake with proper tree ties, not string or rope, as this will cut the tree. Strips of hessian or old cloth about one or two inches wide are suitable, but will eventually rot. The plastic buckle ties are excellent, and the smaller endless loop-lock strips of plastic suitable for smaller trees and shrubs. In windy coastal areas, tree ties must be tied tightly between November and April, to avoid root rocking, thus breaking young roots. In April the ties can be loosened to allow for tree growth.

FEEDING

Unless you are growing dwarf conifers and alpines, and wish to keep them very dwarf, most plants will benefit from a dressing of Growmore fertiliser (about one desert spoonful) sprinkled around them after planting. Sandy and gravelly soils and shallow soils over rock or shale, are all poor soils and definitely need feeding if good growth is to be obtained. Garden compost, well rotted manure, rotted hay or straw and leafmould are all helpful, and can be dug in before planting, or applied as a mulch, or both. To get good growth in sandy soils, two or three applications of Growmore fertilizer may be necessary; at the end of March, the end of May and the last application, the end of July. If shrubs and trees are fed with nitrogenous fertilizers later than July, soft growth may be induced that will get burnt in the winter gales. On average soils, two applications of Growmore will be sufficient, at the end of March and the end of July.

WATERING AND MULCHING

In very windswept and exposed situations spring planting is advisable. Five months of battering winds will have been avoided, and the plant will commence growth immediately in this optimum growing time. Springtime is usually very dry, and this will involve a lot of watering. Conifers must be kept well watered and mulched in their first summer (and preferably their second summer) and the larger the conifer when planted, the greater the need for watering and mulching. When planting large conifers or evergreen shrubs, it is also helpful to spray water over the foliage with a hosepipe, in very hot spells, and during drying northerly and easterly winds. *This is vital* when planting large conifers in February, March or April. Mulching around the base with grass mowings, straw or peat will prevent drying out too fast.

In sandy, gravelly or other well drained soils, or on banks, it helps considerably to leave a shallow depression in the soil, and place the mulch in this. Water will be retained in the saucer-like depression. This idea is most helpful when planting on top of banks.

PEAT LOVING PLANTS

Rhododendrons, Azaleas, Heathers, Andromeda, Pieris, Kalmia and Pernettyas are all lime haters needing acid soil, therefore plenty of peat *must* be placed in the planting hole, *and also* used as a mulch, when any of the above plants are grown. Unless your soil is sand or gravel, heathers will not need to be fertilised with Growmore fertiliser, but bone meal and seaweed meal fertilisers are helpful when planting. Rhododendrons and Azaleas will benefit from an annual mulch of well rotted manure, or bracken or leafmould, as well as the peat dressing.

All these peat lovers however (with the possible exception of heathers) will not flourish in windswept areas, particularly the salty winds, so some kind of shelter must be given to them.

PRUNING AND ETC.

All Hebes (Veronica) and Fuchsias should be tip pruned, or 'pinched back', at planting, and maybe a second tip pruning later on, to induce bushy growth and to avoid legginess. All hedging plants should be tipped back at planting, for the same reason. Leyland cypress and other hedging conifers need not be tipped until they reach the desired height, but the side branches can be pruned. Brooms should be lightly sheared over every year, cutting only the young one year growth, this will keep them bushy. Most silver leaved plants, Senecio, Santolina, Helichrysum, Artemisia, Lavender etc., are far better for hard pruning every year. This also applies to Tree Lupins and the Tree Mallow (Lavatera olbia rosea).

SHRUBS IN GRASS

When trees or shrubs are planted in grass or a lawn, a circular area must be kept clear of weeds and grass around them. Thick mulching with grass mowings will do this, but in a hot summer they will need to be watered well and fed well. Where specimen trees or shrubs are planted in a lawn, another good idea is to leave a circular area three feet in diameter around the plant, ½-1 inch lower than the grass area. Cover this with a piece of thick black polythene, make a few slits in it, (to let the rain through) then cover with small stones or pea size gravel, so that the top of the stones or gravel, are level with the grass.

I have seen numerous examples of conifers, trees and shrubs growing in very exposed situations by the sea, surviving very well, but struggling to grow for the lack of water and food. They were planted in grass which was allowed to remain around them, with the result that in the long hot summer, they are robbed of both food and water by the ravenous grass roots.

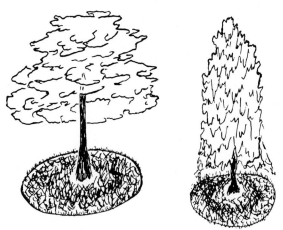

Trees & shrubs planted in grass must be well mulched.

30

CHAPTER 4

Windbreaks and Screens for Exposure

TALL SCREENS AND HEDGES OVER 10 FEET

Whilst the eventual size of the plants listed in this chapter will grow to heights from 10-30 feet, all the deciduous trees can be cut annually and kept at lower heights where desired. With the exception of spruces and pines, all the evergreens listed can likewise be cut.

ACER psuedo-platanus, Sycamore. Excellent deciduous tree for exposed sites and in any soil. This tree is often seen by the coast, and is planted around cottages and farms as a windbreak. Do not plant too near a dwelling house, as it may grow too big and create excessive shade.

ALNUS glutinosa, Common Alder. This deciduous tree will grow in any soil, but thrives and grows fast in moist soils. We planted a mixture of common alder and grey alder, as windbreaks on our nurseries. They have grown exceedingly fast in our wet soil, and stand up to all the gales. We cut ours hard every year, and it is wise to keep the top and sides cut annually from an early age if it is to be used as a hedge.

CUPRESSUS MACROCARPA, Monterey Cypress. If used right on the coast it may get burnt by the salt winds on the seaward side, but will still make a good screen. Hedges less than a mile inland, will thrive near the coast, but too much cutting is not a good thing. Can be damaged by cold and freezing winds.

CUPRESSUS macrocarpa lutea, Golden Monterey Cypress. Both this golden variety and the green one listed above are very fast growers. This golden variety however, is much more wind and salt tolerant.

ELAEAGNUS ebbingei. This has proved to be the most wind and salt tolerant of all the seaside shrubs, and will eventually reach a height of well over ten feet with a spread of ten feet. It is difficult to propogate, hence its comparitive scarcity. Also it does not grow as fast as escallonia or griselinia. This evergreen has glossy green leaves above with silvery undersides, its white flowers are tiny and inconspicuous but are highly scented.

ESCALLONIA, The *Chilean Gum Box.* One of the most widely used evergreen shrubs for seaside hedges. The varieties macrantha, C. F. Ball, Ingramii and Crimson Spire will all grow to a little over 10 feet if left uncut. However, annual cutting after flowering is essential, if a thick hedge is to be created. All have dark green glossy foliage with a rosy red or crimson flowers from May to October.

EUONYMUS japonica, Evergreen Japanese Spindleberry. Survives the severest exposure right on the coast. However it is very slow to grow, and is inclined to lose its deep green colour and become yellowish on poor sandy soils.

FRAXINUS excelsior, Common Ash. This is another deciduous tree found growing a lot on the coast. Like the sycamore it is used to shelter farms and cottages by the sea. It grows fast, tolerates any soil, but thrives in our moist and heavy soil.

GRISELINIA littoralis. This evergreen from the coasts of New Zealand is a wind and salt tolerant plant growing moderately fast, and is useful for screens up to 20 feet. Very tall hedges can be seen right on the coast. Whilst severe winter winds may scorch the young growing tips, it will grow on again quickly in the summer. It has light green leaves and stems.

PICEA sitchensis, Sitka Spruce. This is not the christmas tree with soft green needles, but the tougher version, with sharp, hard, blue-green needles. We have used this as our main windbreak around our nurseries. It is not as fast a grower as Pinus contorta on rich soils, and only does best on moist or heavy soils. It is not suitable for sandy, gravelly or poor soils which dry out much in summer. Our own spruces achieved a height of about 25 feet in 26 years, they can grow faster if weedicides are used to keep grass and weeds down, and irrigation given in a dry summer. They have suffered through the three droughty summers we have just had, and the very many dry springtimes. They are certainly more at home in cool wet summers.

PINUS, The Pines. These conifers are undoubtedly the most widely planted and successful tall trees for seaside areas. They are among the fastest growing and most wind tolerant conifers.

Pinus radiata (insignis) The Monterey Pine grows very fast, with beautiful light green foliage. It is often recommended for coastal planting, however we have found that it is very prone to damage by sea winds in very exposed areas.

Pinus nigra austriaca, Austrian Pine. This tough pine can be recommended for any coastal area, but it is very slow growing.

Pinus contorta, Beach Pine is a very fast growing tree in good soils, it is excellent for coastal exposure, but like all pines is best in sandy, light, poor and well drained soils. If planted in heavy or moist soils, it is inclined to blow over at an angle, but if several trees are planted in a clump, this is not noticable, as the tree straightens itself again.

POPULUS alba, The White or Silver Poplar is the most suitable for seaside exposure, and will quickly form a thicket of growth with its numerous suckers. It can be cut back annually and kept low if desirable.

Populus robusta is a very fast growing tree if planted on moist or heavy soils. It is not advised to plant in extreme exposure, as it will suffer from salt burn. However, it will regrow from the base. It should be sited just a little inland, or given a modicum of protection.

QUERCUS ilex, The Evergreen Oak, or Holm Oak is very resistant to sea winds, is a bushy grower, making a large dense tree, or can be clipped as a hedge. It is a very slow grower, is very difficult to propagate, which makes it scarce and expensive.

SALIX, The Willows are excellent quick growing screens and hedges. We have used these as hedges on our nurseries, as they were very inexpensive and quick to grow. They must be cut back hard every year, otherwise they become too straggly and take up too much room. *Salix alba* the White Willow and *Salix caprea* the Goat Willow are the toughest for coastal exposure. However there are a number of new hybrid willows, all very fast growing, which are worth trying.

SAMBUCUS nigra, The Common Elder will grow in extreme exposure, in any soil, in sun or shade. It does not make a tidy hedge, and hence must be regularly cut to encourage dense growth. The Golden Leaved Elder which is very attractive, is almost as tough.

ULMUS glabra, The Wych Elm or Scotch Elm will tolerate full exposure, but unless cut will make a very large tree. It is quick growing and grows in most soils.

CHAPTER 5

Medium Size Hedges for Exposure

The plants listed in this section will grow from 6-10 feet high, but all can be cut, and kept to a lower height, with the exception of Bamboo, Mountain Pine and the Hardy Palm.

ARUNDINARIA japonica, The *Common Bamboo* will form a suitable shelter in exposed gardens, providing the soil is heavy or moist. It can be badly burnt by the wind, but will regrow in June. This regeneration is possible in established plants. Young plants may require initial protection to get them started. Mulch with well rotted manure or other humus, and water well in drought. It grows from 8-10 feet.

CORDYLINE australis, The *New Zealand Palm* or Hardy Palm is in fact very much hardier than is imagined. Young plants may need a little protection in the winter from frost and N and E winds. Once established it will grow quite quickly if the soil does not dry out too much in the summer. After planting a four year old Cordyline in our nurseries, in rich moist soil, it grew to above ten feet in eight years. Once a trunk develops it will withstand a great degree of exposure in coastal gardens. Mulching with well rotted manure and watering in a drought will be most helpful. Not to be used inland, where 20°F of frost (i.e. 12°F) would kill it.

CYTISUS, The *Hybrid Broom* is a very fast growing flowering shrub that could be used to make very colourful hedges by the sea. It must be grown in sandy, gravelly or any well drained soil, and it lives longer and flowers better in a poorer soil than a rich one. Annual cutting is vital, both to keep it well branched and wind firm, and to prevent it exhausting itself by the

34

production of too much seed. Shears can be used, but cut only into young wood, removing as many seed pods as possible. It grows to 6 feet.

FUCHSIA. Many varieties of Fuchsias can be found growing by the sea, and these make attractive hedges, with very long flowering period. We find that *Fuchsia Mrs. Popple* will flower from July to Christmas, if the winter is mild. *Fuchsia Magellanica alba* with tiny white flowers is the tallest, growing 8-10 feet, and it is the toughest. *Fuchsia Gracilis* and *F. Riccartonii* both with the familiar red and purple flowers grow about six feet. When planting fuchsias, bury them about two inches deeper than the soil ball or pot. It is also helpful in the first year or two, to cover around the stems up to a height of 2-3 inches with gravel, sand or leafmould, in the winter period, in the event of frost. Should the frost be severe the branches above ground may die, but it will regrow from the base in spring, with as much vigour as before, if this precaution is taken.

HIPPOPHAE *rhamnoides, Sea Buckthorn* is an exceedingly tough deciduous shrub which will grow right at the sea edge. It has narrow silver leaves on the thorny stems, and orange berries if male and female plants are used. Suckers quickly spring up from the base making it a very dense impenetrable hedge. It will grow 8-10 feet if not cut.

OLEARIA, The *Daisy Bushes* are amongst the toughest of the seaside shrubs for exposed sites. All are evergreen with silver or grey leaves and white daisy flowers.

O.*Traversii* is the tallest, and is very fast growing, making a very attractive bushy hedge. It does not flower, and is damaged by freezing winds, but will regrow again.

O.*macrodonta* called New Zealand Holly because of its holly-like leaves is another fast growing shrub reaching 6-8 feet and as wide. It should be pruned after flowering to prevent it becoming leggy. O.*albida* with sage green leaves above, buff-silver beneath, stands the full blast of the gales high up on Land's End moor. The flowers quickly turn brown making it look drab and untidy, so should be quickly pruned off. A moderately fast grower reaching 6-8 feet.

PINUS *montana, The Mountain Pine* is a dwarf bushy pine seldom exceeding 8-10 feet in poor sandy or rocky soils. It is clothed to the ground with its stocky, bushy branches. This excellent conifer has been used as a windbreak on the coasts of Denmark, the east coast of Scotland and on a bleak hilltop in North-west Wales. It ought to be used more freely, but because it is a slow grower, is often discarded, in this hurry-worry, time conscious speeded up world.

RIBES, The Flowering Currant is another flowering hedge often seen on the west coast. R.sanguineum with pink and scarlet flowers grows 6-8 feet, and like most seaside hedges, a light pruning after flowering will keep it bushy.

ROSA rugosa scabrosa, this is a specie rose with single mauve-pink flowers followed by very large spectacular hips in the autumn. This rose will come true from its suckers forming a dense screen. It will grow on any soil, even sand, and is immune to mildew and blackspot. Exceptionally hardy and stocky bush growing 6-8 feet.

SPARTIUM junceum, Spanish Broom is a quick growing broom with rush-like stems, and yellow, fragrant flowers, attaining about six feet in average soil conditions. Like all brooms and Genista it must have well drained soil, and lasts longer in poorer soil. In the Mediterranean it can be seen growing at the sea's edge. This is a shrub that must be cut back without fail, after flowering, and will stand quite hard pruning.

TAMARIX, The Tamarisks are to be seen all along the coast, in many countries, standing wind and salt spray, and capable of living in pure sand by the sea. Tall and sparse, with feathery foilage and pink plumes, tamarisks grow 8-10 feet. Natives of sands and deserts, they will not thrive in heavy or wet soils. Prune hard in April otherwise they will become very leggy.

CHAPTER 6

Low Hedges for Exposure

The plants listed here will grow from 3-5 feet, in very rich soils they may exceed this. However, all are better for a light pruning, and this will keep them down.

CEANOTHUS, The *Californian Lilac* is a very large family, from the totally prostrate to those that will climb up a house. They provide us with the best blue flowered shrubs, which are hardy outdoors. *C.thyrsiflorus repens* with small, glossy, dark green leaves and blue flower puffs in the spring, stands up to the wind quite well in our nurseries. It must have a sunny situation and well drained soil, and grows quickly to a height of 4-5 feet and spreading much more than this sideways.

CISTUS, The *Sun Roses* coming from the Mediterranean region, succeed best in poor dry soil, in full sun. Good drainage is vital for all the mediterranean plants, otherwise they perish in the winter. C.laurifolius is the toughest and tallest with dark green gummy leaves and white flowers. It will attain a height of 4-5 feet and similar width. Three others could be tried, *C.cyprius* with white flowers blotched maroon, 4 feet, *C.corbariensis* with white flowers, 3-4 feet, and *C.crispus* with rose-pink flowers, 2-3 feet.

FUCHSIAS. We have already dealt with the taller fuchsias more suited to medium sized hedges, but there are dozens of low growing fuchsias, unfortunately most of these are not hardy. *F.gracilis variegata* has pink, cream and green variegated leaves, and the usual red and purple flowers. This will make the most unusual and attractive hedge. Cut back to ground level any branches that revert back to plain green. For planting instructions, refer to Chapter 5. "Fuchsias". Fuchsia pumilia is a dwarf version of F.riccartonii, growing only 1½-2 ft, but very hardy, and will re-grow from ground level.

HEBE. The Veronicas are a very varied and colourful race of evergreen shrubs that thrive by the sea. It must be emphasised at the outset, that whilst several of these Veronicas withstand a great deal of exposure both to wind and salt, they are not tough enough to withstand severe freezing winds, which regrettably blow up quite unexpectedly, and have occured these past 4 or 5 years. This applies mainly to very young plants, older plants may regrow from the base. *H.franciscana Blue Gem* with violet-blue flower, and flowering on and off not only throughout the summer, but in midwinter also, makes a compact dome 5 feet x 5 feet, and is the toughest. There is also a pretty little dwarfer variety of this same plant, H.franciscana variegata with cream and green variegated leaves, but no flowers. It is equally hardy, and reaches two feet. The Veronicas can be had with a variety of flowers, in white, pink, red, blue, mauve and purple, but none of these other varieties can be recommended unreservedly for the first line of defence. They will however be perfectly at home behind a hedge or some situation a little sheltered from the worst of the wind. All Veronicas prefer a sunny position and dislike cold and wet, so make sure the soil is well drained if you wish them to thrive.

HELICHRYSUM rosmarinifolius, this is a very solid, compact little shrub, attaining 4-5 feet, with dark green narrow, rosemary-like leaves and crimson flower buds which eventually fade to white. A very striking shrub when in flower, this Tasmanian plant was called "Snow in Summer." It requires a sunny position and good drainage.

LYCIUM chinese, "Duke of Argyll's Tea Tree", a vigorous shrub with spiny arching stems, flowering June-September, followed by orange or scarlet berries. We have found this growing at the edge of the sea, in Cardigan Bay. It grows 4-6 feet and it is reputed to stand the fiercest of gales, even on the cliff tops of N. Yorkshire.

OLEARIA. The taller varieties of Daisy Bushes have been dealt with in Chapter 4. *O.Haastii* has small, shining, grey-green box-like leaves and small white daisy flowers, it grows to four feet. *O.gunniana* with soft, dark, grey-green foilage is exceptionally lovely in flower, it can flower so profusely, that no leaves are visible. It makes a compact upright bush of 4-5 feet.

ROSMARINUS, The Common Rosemary is another shrub from the Mediterranean countries where it can be found right on the cliffs by the sea, with its pleasantly fragrant leaves and pale blue flowers. It dislikes cold winters and heavy soil, thriving as it does in sunny situations, in sandy or light, well drained soil. Likewise, it will not tolerate N or E or other bleak situations.

SENECIO greyii, another of the tough seaside shrubs from the coasts of New Zealand, well adapted to withstand both Pacific and Atlantic gales . It has silver-grey leaves and yellow, daisy-like flowers, it grows to a height of 3-4 feet and similar spread. Young plants must be tip pruned frequently to encourage bushiness.

ULEX europaeus, Common Gorse abounds all over Britain, and can be seen in the most exposed positions on the cliffs by the sea. Its yellow flowers can be seen throughout most of the year. Best in poor soil and sunny situations. They can be pruned hard after flowering if necessary.

CHAPTER 7

Shrubs for Moderate Exposure

The following shrubs are not recommended for very exposed gardens by the sea, but only for gardens possessing a degree of shelter from the worst winds, or sites sufficiently far enough from the coast.

ARBUTUS unedo, The Strawberry Tree is a native woodland plant in Kerry, Ireland. It is an evergreen upright bush or small tree, with red-brown trunk and cream-white heath-like waxy bells in autumn, and one year later gives a crop of round, rough textured orange and yellow fruit. Plant in pairs for cross pollination. The fruit is insipid.

BERBERIS stenophylla, This evergreen Barberry has numerous, slender, arching branches clothed with small, dark green, narrow foliage and clusters of apricot yellow flowers in spring. It is best if pruned hard after flowering to keep it shapely and to encourage young basal growth. *B.darwinii* with small holly-like leaves and orange flowers, is much more popular, but because of its somewhat wider leaf is definitely more susceptible to winds, particularly cold winds.

BUDDLEIA, The Butterfly Bush. All the Buddleias thrive near the sea, and *B.davidii* varieties can be had with purple, red, blue and white flowers, and growing 6-8 feet. These must be cut back hard to within 12 inches of the soil each year between November and April, if very windy, choose the earlier date. *B.alternifolia* a graceful willowy shrub with arching branches with small, silver-grey foliage and lavender honey scented flowers borne in little clusters along yard long shoots in early June. This must not be pruned hard, only a light trimming after flowering. It grows 6-10 feet, and is most spectacular trained as a standard, when it becomes a flowering weeping tree. *B.globosa, The Chilean Orange Ball Tree* with olive green semi-evergreen foliage and bears clustered ball-like orange flowers in May and June. This buddleia must not be pruned hard every year, only a light trimming after flowering. However it is a very fast grower, and may quickly get out of hand, in which case prune back to 12 inches from soil level. In some parts it does withstand full coastal exposure.

CASSINIA fulvida is mis-called "The Golden Heather" on account of its gold heath-like foliage and stems. It bears small white flowers in July, which quickly brown, so should be pruned over, to tidy it and keep it shapely. This New Zealand evergreen could be tried in more exposed areas, but it dislikes freezing winds.

CORTADERIA argentea, Pampas Grass will grow satisfactorily by the sea, but requires good shelter from the wind on account of its tall white plumes, which appear August-October. We find in our windswept nurseries, that this is just the time when strong winds begin, thus laying flat all the tall stately wands, and creating a scene of chaos, thereby destroying the principal beauty of the plant. However, there is a dwarfer version called Cortaderia pumila which can be tried.

COTONEASTER bullatus usually grown as a small tree 10-12 feet can also be grown as a shrub, when it would be a little smaller. It has large, interesting corrugated leaves followed by red berries, and brilliant autumn colour. *C.franchetii* is a smaller, semi-evergreen with small greyish foliage and orange scarlet berries, it grows to 6 feet. *C.microphylla* this small, glossy leaved evergreen from the Himalayas, has large red berries, and is extremely tough, can be found on windswept hills facing the sea. Unfortunately it is a low growing cotoneaster, hardly reaching two feet, but with a very large spread. It can be used to climb up banks or cascade down low walls.

CUPRESSOCYPARIS leylandii. This conifer has the reputation of being the fastest growing of all conifers, and on our nurseries we have made 24 feet of growth in 8 years. However, we do have rich, moist soil. If it is to make maximum growth and also to avoid any browning and loss of foliage, it must be kept moist in summer, either by watering or mulching, or both, during the first year or two of its life. In a planting trial right by the sea, in a very exposed situation, we found that *C.leylandii* was burnt almost to the ground, in the winter, but did regrow from the base in the summer. For this reason, we do not recommend it for right on or near the shore-line. It does need to be placed a little more inland or given a little protection. *C.leylandii Robinson's Gold* is a comparatively new golden version of the aforementioned green leylandii, and has all the attributes of the same including speed of growth. It is too early to assess its hardiness to sea winds, but I would hazard a guess that it may prove to be a little more hardy than the green leylandii. Both these cypresses can have their tops and sides trimmed at any age, but it is wiser not to continually cut back the top in the same place every year.

ELAEAGNUS pungens maculata. The Golden variegated elaeagnus may be just as hardy in very exposed positions, as the green E.ebbingei, but it is listed here with shrubs for moderate exposure, on account of its slow growth. This really is a most spectacular and beautiful shrub with its polished leaves flecked with yellow, gold and green, and it is a pity to slow down its growth rate even more so, by planting it in difficult positions. Its eventual size may be over six feet, but it will take a very long time to reach this height.

GENISTA hispanica, Spanish Gorse is extremely wind hardy, but its low height of only about two feet, makes it of little use as a hedge. It makes a dense hummock of prickly green, completely smothered in May and June with yellow flowers. It will grow in pure sand close to the sea, tolerates acid or alkaline soils, thrives in sun and really poor soils, and like Cytisus and Spartium must have good drainage.

HYDRANGEAS thrive well by the sea, due to the comparative freedom from frost. So try to avoid a frost pocket, otherwise the young soft growth in the spring will be burnt. They like rich, moist soil, but also need good drainage, so add plenty of well rotted manure or other humus, when planting. An acid soil produces blue flowers, and an alkaline soil pink or red flowers. The white flowered kinds do not depend on acidity or alkalinity. All prefer moist soil, but red varieties tolerate more drought and sun, and pale blue and white will grow to perfection in partial shade. Hydrangeas are best left unpruned, merely cutting off dead flower stalks. They grow from 3-4 feet. These foregoing remarks refer to the common hydrangea macrophylla and not to H.villosa or H.paniculata grandiflora which grow much taller.

HYPERICUM hidcote, The Shrubby St. John's Wort is one of the best ever-green shrubs easily grown, with large golden flowers from July to

October, making a dome about four feet high, and tolerant of poor dry soil. Pruning consists merely in the removal of branch ends that have flowered. It can occasionally be hard pruned back, if it gets straggly, and then it regrows into a dense bush.

LABURNUM, The *Golden Chain* is a small tree attaining about 12 feet in ten years. It can be seen growing wild in some farm hedges by the sea, and in exposed places. *L.vossii* with its long golden racemes, is the best variety for its profusion and length of flower racemes. Laburnums will not tolerate wet or heavy soil, thriving best in light well drained soils.

LAVATERA olbia rosea, The *Tree Mallow* is a very fast growing useful shrub, covered in deep pink flowers from July to October, and even later in mild winters. It quickly reaches five feet, but should be cut back to at least half its height, in winter to avoid being blown over in the winter gales. Though short lived, its quick growth, profusion of flowers and tolerance of sea winds, make it a very desirable shrub for coastal gardens.

LAVANDULA, The *Lavenders* thrive in hot, dry sunny positions by the coast, doing best in poor soils, even pure sand. They will not succeed in moist or heavy soils. The dwarf varieties grow 1½ feet and the tall to 3 feet.

LUPINUS arborea, The *Tree Lupin* like the tree mallow, is another fast growing, and profusely flowering shrub, quickly attaining five feet. The hybrids come in a variety of colours and are scented. It grows best in poor, light or sandy soils, and though short lived, is another very rewarding shrub for the coast.

PEROVSKIA atriplicifolia, The *Afghan Sage* with its finely cut grey leaves and lavender-blue flowers, is a most striking and beautiful shrub for a sunny situation and light soil. Cut back hard each spring. It will grow to three feet.

PHLOMIS fruticosa. The *Jerusalem Sage* with large, soft, grey leaves and golden heads of whorled flowers in June and July grows 3-4 feet. It withstands quite a lot of salt winds by the sea. Another Mediterranean shrub needing light soil and full sun.

PHORMIUM tenax, The *New Zealand Flax* is valued for its striking architectural effect in the garden, with its erect, evergreen sword-like leaves growing 6-8 feet in good rich soil. This is another tough wind resister, which will grow in pure sand, but it makes its maximum growth in moist heavier soils. It produces flowers in huge tall, primordial-like stalks, which, whilst a curiosity, are ungainly and not particularly attractive. There is also a purple leaved variety, growing to the same size, and hybrids in white, cream and gold variegation.

PITTOSPORUM tenuifolium is an Australian evergreen with pale green, shiny rippled leaves and black stems, and is so beloved by florists for floral decoration. Thriving best in light soils, it will also grow in other soils, providing they are not waterlogged in winter. It needs protection from N and E winds. In good situations by the coast it grows from 6-8 feet and has tiny, inconspicuous flowers honey scented. *P.tenuifolium Garnettii* is a pretty variegated version of the foregoing with white variegated leaves turning pink in winter. It is not quite as tough as P.tenuifolium, and both shrubs may get their tips burnt with cold N and E winds. They will however, grow away happily in the spring, if the plants are well established.

SANTOLINA incana, The *Cotton Lavender* will thrive in extreme exposure to salt-laden winds and in dry, sandy or poor soils. It has aromatic silvery foliage and gold button-like flowers in July and August. Cut back hard after flowering, to keep it compact, and avoid straggly growth. Best in sunny positions. It is 1½-2 feet. There is a very finely cut leaf variety S.neapolitana, and a green leaf variety S.virens.

SORBRUS aria, The *Whitebeam* is the best of the Sorbrus family for sea-side exposure, reaching 15-18 feet in ten years on good soil. It grows in any soil, but resents waterlogging. It has leaves whose upper surface is green and the underside is white, and has berries in the autumn, and is very hardy and resistant to wind.

S.aucuparia, The *Mountain Ash* or Rowan is another small tree with pinnate leaves and very showy scarlet berries in the autumn. Because of its tendency to branch out from the base, it can be grown as a shrub, by tipping the leader occasionally.

CHAPTER 8

Within the Shelter

Once a windbreak or hedge has become established around your seaside garden your growing potential is now limited only by your soil, situation and determination! It should be remembered at the outset that whilst rhododendrons, azaleas and other peat-loving subjects do thrive near the coast, the following cultural instructions are vital.

PEAT LOVERS

Rhododendrons, azaleas, Pieris, Magnolias, Camellias, Mahonia, Pernettya, Kalmia and Skimmias all require protection from wind and benefit from partial shade. Without these two factors, it is useless to try to grow the above plants. Whilst azaleas, rhododendrons, pernettya, pieris and kalmia all demand a lime free soil and the addition of peat. All the above nine subjects will flourish in a rich, well drained soil with abundant humus. Should this latter be lacking, it can be made good by the generous use of coarse peat, and the addition of Growmore fertiliser added in April and July at 1-2 ounces per square yard (or one desertspoonful per plant). Seaweed Meal fertiliser added at 8 ounces per square yard, is another very good soil improver, as it is rich in all minerals and trace elements.

Nothing can be more showy and dazzling in April and May, than a rich display of the various coloured large flowering rhododendrons and deciduous azaleas. The dwarf Japanese azaleas and dwarf rhododendrons, are equally colourful, even though smaller in flower. Then add the camellias and magnolias, and the brilliant red leaves of Pieris forrestii and you get a brilliant canvas of breathtaking beauty. But, to add a regrettably

45

sad, but necessary note, these plants (excluding the dwarf rhododendrons and azaleas) all grow to above five feet eventually, and in rich soils maybe over ten feet. This means they need either a sheltered site, or tall hedges.

Kalmias must be treated like the large growing rhododendrons, but they are much slower growing. Their unbelievably beautiful pink flowers, glistening like some fantastic floral icing on a cake, regrettably are not as easy to grow as rhododendrons, hence their scarcity.

Mahonia bealei. M.japonica and M.lomariifolia flower in the period November to January, and therefore need shelter particularly from north and east. Their sweetly scented yellow flowers will go unnoticed in a windy garden, and their large architecturally beautiful leaves will be burnt and damaged if subject to much wind.

Pernettya mucronata are the showiest of all dwarf berrying evergreens, making dense thickets about three feet high. The small white flowers are followed by clusters of very long lasting, marble-like berries in white, pink, red, mauve and purple, and often ignored by the birds. They need a lime free soil, with the addition of peat. One male plant to 4-6 females, is necessary to ensure a good display of berries.

Skimmia japonica is a slow growing compact evergreen thriving in shady situations. It has creamy white flower clusters, delicately fragrant, followed by large holly-like berries in the autumn, if there is a male planted in the group. The male form is *S.japonica rubella* with larger and more conspicuous flowers, carries its red buds in late winter, opening to pink in the spring.

Pruning should not be necessary for azaleas, rhododendrons or camellias, unless over-feeding with nitrogenous fertilisers, or growing in over rich soil has occured, or the plants may have grown too large. In any case, loss of flowers must be expected for a year or two. However, rhododendrons and azaleas should be 'dead headed' or the careful removal of flower stalks as soon as the flowers have faded, to prevent seed formation which inhibits bud formation. A dressing of bone meal, well rotted manure and peat should then be given, and the plants watered if the weather is very dry. Likewise, camellias, magnolias and pieris should be mulched in spring with a generous supply of peat, to keep the soil moist and cool, and watered in a drought. With all the peat loving plants, no soil disturbance should be practised once the plants are established. Hence the land should be free of perennial weeds before planting.

46

In a windswept garden by the sea, where tall hedges are impossible or undesirable, then the dwarf evergreen *Japanese azaleas* are a good choice. They come in many colours, in various shades of white, red, pink, violet, purple and orange, and grow two to three feet high but spread well. Better still for this windy garden are the *Dwarf and Alpine Rhododendrons* such as *R.Cowslip* with cream and pink flowers, and its height and spread is 4 x 4 feet. *R.Humming Bird* with deep rosy bell-shaped flowers, size 3 x 3 feet. *R.Elizabeth* with large scarlet bells, size 3 x 3 feet. *R.Blue Tit* with clear blue flowers, size 3 x 3 feet. *R.Chikor* with yellow flowers, size 2 x 2 feet. *R.Keleticum* has deep purple flowers with crimson spots, size 6 x 12 inches. *R.Radicans* a totally prostrate little rhododendron with rich purple flowers, that will creep and spread over rocks. Here then are just a few of a very large collection of hardy rhododendrons, which by their very low size are more easily managed in a windy seaside garden, and demand only a low hedge, or a group of evergreen shrubs to windward. Like the tall rhododendrons and azaleas, removal of dead flower heads, a good mulch of peat, and watering during a drought is the best treatment during the summer. They will tolerate much poorer soil than the tall growing rhododendrons, and will tolerate much more sun. However, if it is not possible to give any shade, in a long hot summer, the flowers do not last long, and quickly loose their brightness of colour.

HEATHERS AND TREE HEATHERS

All heathers do best in a lime free soil, but *Erica terminalis*, *E.mediterranea*, *E.carnea* and *The Winter Flowering Hybrids*, all with tolerate some lime in the soil, so long as it is not pure chalk! The soil should be friable, or made so by the admixture of plenty of humus, and maybe plenty of grit as well, if it is very heavy soil or clay. It should not be waterlogged. If drainage is not possible, it can be raised, six or twelve inches higher than the surrounding soil. Heathers should be in as open and sunny a position as possible, and should not be under the drips from trees. A generous amount of peat should be spread around each heather at planting, and a mulch of peat spread all over the surface of the heather bed. Heathers do not need a rich soil or feeding, once they are established. On sands, gravels and other definitely poor soils, bonemeal and Growmore fertilisers maybe necessary at planting, and in the first year or two. On these poor soils it is better to give the soil a good dressing of well rotted manure or well made compost before planting. Apart from an annual dressing of peat, all over the surface in spring, the only other necessity, is to shear over the plants after flowering.

Nothing could be less trouble free and more satisfying throughout the whole of the year than a garden bed laid out with a good selection of heathers, tree heathers and the occasional dwarf conifer. Do not plant heathers in single plants of one kind. A much better effect is produced by planting 5-8 plants of one variety together in a mass. Vary the colours, and choose varieties of different heights, thus producing an evergreen ground cover that is not monotonous, but of interest at all seasons. To produce a calender of bloom from January to December, and to use the plants as ground cover, varying the heights, colours and textures, to produce a colourful tapestry of perennial interest, the following is a suggestion for a bed six feet wide and twenty-four feet long.

Species and varieties	No.	Description	Flowering	Height ins.
Winterfl. hyb. Ghost Hills	5	pink	Dec.-April	18
Winterfl. hyb. Silver Beads	5	white	Dec.-April	18
E.carnea Eileen Porter	5	carmine	Oct.-April	9
E.carnea Lesley Sparkes	5	gold fol. pink fl.	Dec.-Feb.	9
E.carnea Springwood White	5	white	Jan.-Mar.	9
E.carnea Vivellii	5	dark carmine	Feb.-Mar.	9
E.Mediterranea alba	1	white	Feb.-April	36
E.Mediterranea superba	1	rosy pink	Mar.-May*	48
E. Australis riverslea	1	deep rosy red	April-June	72
Daboecia alba	5	white	June-Oct.	24
Daboecia pink	5	white with pink	June-Sept.	15
Daboecia Wm. Buchanan	5	rose red	May-Oct.	9
E.Cinerea alba major	5	white	July-Aug.	9
E.Cinerea atro. sang. Reuthe's	5	deep carmine	July-Aug.	6
E.Cinerea pink ice	5	soft pink	June-Sept.	9

Juniper chinensis Stricta, a symmetrical pyramid of bright blue grey foliage: 3-5 feet.

Thuja occidentalis Rheingold, a rounded compact bush of gold foliage: 3 ft.

New varieties and hybrids, are constantly being offered, including many useful dwarf varieties.

48

This book is not intended to be a catalogue of plants and their cultivation, but primarily a list of trees and shrubs for coastal gardens. It is also attempting to show that, with some measure of protection from the worst sea winds, there are good possibilities for growing tender and unusual shrubs and trees in gardens by the sea. The ordinary run-of-the-mill, or well known deciduous shrubs, are therefore not mentioned, since they will grow almost anywhere, and do not need the same degree of protection. However, no garden is complete without them, and they are useful in coastal gardens as "nurse plants" for tender shrubs, by planting a group of these tougher shrubs to windward. The following, are suggested as a few of the more choice shrubs and trees that can be attempted.

ABELIA grandiflora. This semi-evergreen of hybrid origin, is a reasonably hardy member of a family of aristocratic shrubs worth greater attention. The blossoms are pale pink lasting from June to October, and the small leaves brightly coloured, and very useful as cut sprays for vases. It grows to four feet.

ACER palmatum atropurpureum. This Japanese Maple has exceptionally rich purple leaves, which are its main attraction. It is a very beautiful shrub, and grows 6-8 feet, but is a very slow grower. It is used on very large rockeries, or as a lawn specimen, or among heathers. The leaves can be damaged by wind or frost and excessive sunshine. Light dappled shade being best. It needs a well drained friable loam with peat added, and a good mulch of leafmould, compost or old manure. *A.palmatum dissectum atropurpureum*, is an even more striking, but much smaller shrub, very slowly growing to about three feet. It has bronzy crimson leaves that are very finely cut, and a most attractive weeping habit. This shrub must also be protected from winds, frost and excessive sun.

CERCIS siliquastrum, The *Judas Tree* is a spreading bush or small tree growing 10-12 feet. This lovely and most unusual tree has magenta-pink, pea-shaped flowers on naked boughs in May. The heart shaped leaves come after the flowers, and in some parts turn golden in the autumn. It needs very sunny situations, good drainage, and resents pruning. Poor soils are better than over-rich ones.

GARRYA elliptica, The *Californian Catkin Bush*, is a strong growing evergreen with leathery leaves and 9-12 inch grey catkins on male plants, shorter ones, but just as showy on female plants. More successful on S and

W walls, but will grow in partial shade. It is tougher than is supposed, and will stand salt winds, but not the cold winds from N or E. In well sheltered areas it grows strongly and vigorously in the open. However, in a very wet winter with occasional hard frosts, we have found that young plants do get damaged.

HAMAMELIS mollis, The Chinese Witch Hazel is the best of witch hazels. Its spidery golden yellow, highly fragrant flowers, lasting from December to February, are resistant to most weather, including a little frost. Since however it is grown for its delicate beauty of flower and fragrance, it is obviously best to give it good shelter. They prefer soils rich in humus, and in a cool situation. The hazel like foliage gives good autumn colour.

MYRTUS communis, The Common Myrtle has white flowers July-September and aromatic leaves when crushed. It will grow in the open in sheltered gardens by the sea, but inland would need a south wall. *M.communis tarentina, The Dwarf Myrtle* has smaller leaves, is much more wind hardy and has more aromatic leaves.

M.luma, The Chilean Tree Myrtle is undoubtedly one of the few very choice shrubs, that can be grown by the coast. In our nurseries, M.luma reached a height of 16 feet and spread of 10-12 feet in 14 years, which is good growth for the myrtle. Because I did not know at the time of planting, that it would grow so tall, I left it quite unpruned. It had now developed eight trunks spreading outwards from the ground. From August to October it has white scented flowers, followed by black berries. Its very special beauty however, is its trunk, with smooth cinnamon-brown bark, that peels to show the lighter, creamier coloured inner surface.

OSMANTHUS delavayii is another choice evergreen with small, very dark green shiny leaves and small fragrant white flowers in April and May. It grows to six feet and maybe more in width. This graceful shrub with arching growths should be given some protection from late frosts and early morning sun. Dappled shade or half shade may suit it best.

PYRUS salicifolia pendula, The Weeping Silver Pear, grows 15-20 feet in sheltered gardens. This most elegant and attractive small tree has silvery, willow like leaves on weeping branches, and white flowers. A most unusual sight when fully grown, with it pendulous branches arching to the ground. Sunny, well drained sites are best.

ROBINIA psuedoacacia Frisia, The Golden False Acacia, raised in Holland in

1935, is still a comparitively new tree, but quickly gaining in popularity. They grow 20-30 feet in good soil, but can be kept smaller and compact, by judicious pruning, if necessary. It has striking golden foliage, dainty, almost fern-like, from spring until autumn. This feature makes it a very desirable ornamental tree. It needs protection from winds, and light or well drained soil and sunny position.

VIBURNUM. The viburnums are a very large family of easily cultivated shrubs, but I will only deal here with six of them. *V.bodnantense* is a deciduous shrub and a vigorous growing hybrid reaching 6-8 feet, with pink buds opening to white, very fragrant flowers October to December. A most useful shrub to have, flowering as it does, when apart from heathers, there is very little else in flower at this time.

V. burkwoodii is a very attractive evergreen hybrid, with fragrant white flowers on slender arching branches during April and May. It grows 6 feet high and the same in width. *V.fragrans* is a strong growing deciduous shrub growing to 10 feet, with blush pink, sweetly scented flowers on leafless twigs from November to March. It may take a few years to flower freely. *V.tinus Laurustinus* is an excellent seaside evergreen from the Mediterranean. Unlike all the other viburnums mentioned here, it stands a great deal of wind from the sea, and is the easiest to grow. With its compact dense growth, and four inch heads of pink bud clusters opening to white, from October to March, it is another useful winter flowering shrub.

V.tomentosum mariesii is a deciduous shrub with wide spreading branches in horizontal tiers, covered all along the upper sides, in May and June, with white lace-cap flowers, giving the appearance of a snow-laden bush. It grows 4-5 feet, and its leaves turn ruby crimson in the autumn. *V.tomentosum lanarth* is a stronger growing type than V.mariesii, similar, but with larger leaves. It too has good autumn colour. These latter two shrubs grow better in half shade.

HEDGES AND ARBOURS

With small gardens, a single hedge around the entire garden may be all that is possible, but with larger gardens, smaller hedges within the garden, and tall clumps of shrubs or groups of small trees, will also be desirable to check the turbulence of the wind, some distance from the boundary hedge or screen. The landscaping of a large garden can therefore be made to fit into the need for further hedges or wind barriers, as in the sketch. This garden is 100 feet wide and 150 feet long, the house facing SW with wonderful sea views, but very exposed to the wind. A solution is suggested here, by keeping the seaward hedge of elaeagnus ebbingei to five feet, thus preserving the sea view. The strong sea winds are checked by the clump of pines and silver poplars, and the clump of mixed shrubs, as well as the two hedges.

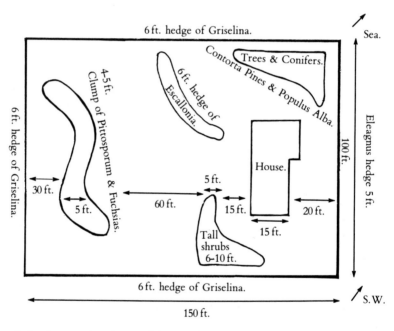

A plan for a 100 ft. wide × 150 ft. long garden, wishing to preserve the sea view from the house, but sheltering the garden.

With gardens of this size or larger, it is possible to create very sheltered sun traps, and cosy arbours and retreats, by the use of hedges, planted to create 'outdoor rooms' as in the sketch. This garden is 100 feet long and 80 feet wide, in a very formal style. Again, the sea view is preserved by keeping a lower hedge around the house to five feet high. By the central positioning of the house, and the semi-circular Fuchsia hedge to within five feet from the house walls, the front garden thus becomes four individual gardens, a, b, c and d. In the three remaining gardens, e, f and g, the object was to achieve total shelter and privacy.

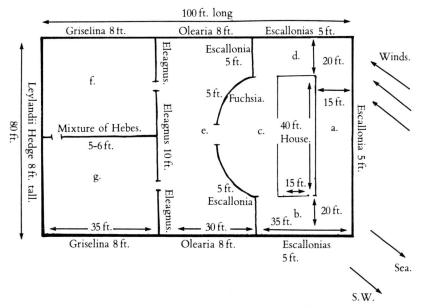

An exposed seaside garden, where the sea-view is retained in all the 4 small gardens around the house. a.b.c.d. In the three remaining gardens e.f.g. the object was to achieve total shelter and privacy.

Another way to create shelter is to dig out a hollow, and spread the soil to windward, making a semi-circular bank. If the hollow is three feet deep and the bank created is two feet, a very cosy sitting or sunbathing area is achieved. Needless to say, the soil must be free draining, or on a slight slope, in order to prevent the hollow becoming a pond in winter! Furthermore, on these banks can be planted a whole variety of alpines and other dwarf shrubs, such as cistus, helichrysum, salvias, cheiranthus, prostrate brooms, genistas and hosts of other sun lovers, that will benefit from the improved drainage achieved by building up the soil into a bank.

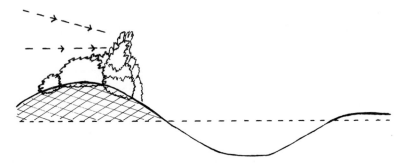

Dig out a hollow 3 ft. deep, and build up a bank 2 ft. high on the windward side. The soil must be free draining or drained with pipes.

CHAPTER 9

Utilising Walls, Buildings, Banks and Raised Beds

If the garden is comparitively flat, in a windswept position near the sea, but a tall barrier around the boundary is not wanted, then use can be made of the walls of the house, buildings and banks to give protection to plants.

N AND E FACING WALLS

These are the most difficult situations for any plants, but the following can be tried.

SELF CLINGING CLIMBERS. Virginia Creeper (Ampelopsis veitchii) and *the ivies* (Hedera) grow well in this situation. The green leaved ivies are the toughest, but depending on the degree of exposure, *Hedera canariensis* vareigata the Canary Island Ivy, *H.colchica dentata aurea* the Perisan Ivy and *H.Jubilee* or Gold Heart could all be tried, but would not succeed if the situation was ravaged by cold N and E winds. In the latter case, only Virginia Creeper and Common green ivy would succeed.

FOR TRELLIS OR WIRES. Jasmine nudiflorum. The Winter Jasmine with yellow flowers on the young green, but leafless shoots, from November to February, is a tough climber for N and E walls. Prune well when young, to encourage plenty of branches, and keep the old wood cut out. *Lonicera periclymenum belgica*, The Early Dutch Honeysuckle with creamy yellow flowers flushed with crimsons, is also a tough climber and strong grower. *Pyracantha gibbsii*, The Firethorn is an evergreen with dark green leaves and tiny hawthorn-like flowers in spring, which often

55

completely cover the entire bush. A tough seaside plant, with very vigorous growth, capable of covering a very large area very prolific scarlet berries in the autumn. Very striking.

WALL SHRUBS THAT CAN BE TRAINED. Cotoneaster horizontalis, The Herring Bone Cotoneaster is a very popular shrub for walls, needing no tying or support, since it grows flat against the wall, with its fan like growth. It berries profusely and its leaves turn scarlet in the autumn. *Elaeagnus ebbingei*, an evergreen with glossy dark green leaves with silver undersides, is among the toughest of seaside plants. It is useful to train against a wall on account of its tiny inconspicuous flowers which are sweetly scented, however it will need a good deal of constant pruning to keep it in place. *Forsythia* is a March flowering shrub with yellow flowers, very easy to grow and tolerant of most soils. Try F.Beatrix Farrand it has exceptionally large flowers. Prune hard after flowering to prevent it becoming too large, cut the older and weaker branches.

WEST FACING WALLS

Ceanothus, The Californian Lilac has a great number of varieties. Among the strong growers that will reach up to the roof if required, are *C.thyrsiflorus, C.dentatus* and *C.Autumn Blue*.

Choisya ternata, The Mexican Orange Blossom is an evergreen that quickly grows into a rounded bush about five feet high. It has clusters of white, fragrant flowers in May and June. These have truly the real orange blossom scent, and sometimes flower again in the autumn. A very rewarding shrub.

Cydonia or *Chaenomeles*, The Flowering Quince is a very tough shrub with flowers ranging from white, orange, pink to red. Flower buds grow thickest on old wood, so once the basic shape or coverage has been achieved, cut back young growth to 4 or 5 inches in late summer. The fruits can be made into jellies.

Escallonia has previously been mentioned under "Windbreaks and Screens", but there are three shorter varieties suitable for training or growing against a wall.

E.Apple Blossom with pink and white chalice-shaped flowers, and growing to four feet.

E.compacta coccinea a very neat grower with small glossy leaves and crimson flowers, it grows to five feet. *E.Donard Seedling* has small leaves

56

Hebe Purple Queen.

Buddleia Davidii.

57

Cotoneaster horizontalis.

Olearia macrodonta, Cassinia fulvida and Cotoneaster microphylla.

Cupressocyparis Leylandii.

Genista hispanica and Aubrieta.

59

Phormium tenax.

Sorbus aria lutescens.

Alpine Bed showing Calceolaria integrifolia and Mexican Salvia.

Callistemon rigidus showing abundance of seed heads.

Crinodendron hookerianum.

Phlomis fruticosa and Geranium, above are Fuchsia.

Golden Privet.

Juniper Hibernica, Thuja, Rhinegold, Erica, Med. Superba, with Cordyine in distance.

Senecio greyii.

Lavender.

and arching branches, and flowers flesh pink in bud, opening to white, and growing to five feet.

Euonymus japonica either the silver variegated, or the gold euonymus is suitable, and grow 4-5 feet.

Lonicera japonica Halliana, the evergreen japanese honeysuckle with fragrant creamy white flowers changing to yellow in June-September. A very strong grower for wires, netting or trellis.

Lonicera japonica aurea reticulata, The Evergreen Golden Honeysuckle has small green leaves patterned with gold veining, and turning pink or purple in the winter. It rarely flowers, but is a strong grower and very colourful climber, for wires, netting or trellis.

Polygonum baldschuanicum, The Russian Vine or "Mile a minute" is the fastest climber for covering walls, tanks, old tree stumps, derelict buildings etc. It has numerous white flowers, and has good autumn colour. Netting or trellis is required for this very vigorous shrub.

SOUTH FACING WALLS

It is not necessary to catalogue the plants that will grow on a south wall, they are legïon! However, all plants listed under N, E and W facing walls will grow just as happily on south facing walls. But on such very warm and sunny walls, Wisteria, Summer Jasmine, Jasmine revolutum, Clematis and Garrya are some very interesting and special plants. For seaside gardens, with comparative absence of frost, the south wall is a wonderful opportunity to grow the unusual or exotic shrubs and climbers, from Australia, New Zealand, Chile and the Mediterranean. These are listed in Chapter 10.

BANKS AND RAISED BEDS

Where there are banks with south facing sides, these can be used for growing smaller shrubs which, whilst difficult or impossible to grow in the rest of the windy garden, will benefit from the warmth and sun that the south banks afford. Should there be no banks, it is easy enough to make a raised bed or 'rockeries', with or without retaining walls.

On our nurseries, we have a long ugly concrete block wall that is the retaining wall for three bunkers, holding sand, gravel and washed stones. This wall faces south so we built another low wall, about 14 inches out from it, and only one concrete block high. The bed is 32 feet long, about 9-

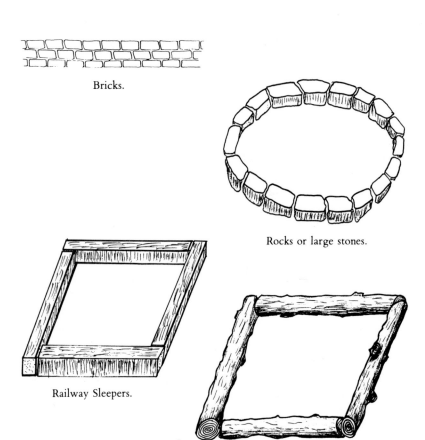

Bricks.

Rocks or large stones.

Railway Sleepers.

Uncut logs.

Drystone walling — shingles.
                  — stones.

10 inches deep and about 14 inches wide. It sits on an existing concrete path, so weep holes were left in the blocks, as they were cemented together, for drainage. This was filled with a mixture of equal parts of soil, grit and peat.

From May to September this is a highly colourful bed, containing dwarf shrubs and a few alpines. It grows plants very successfully, that in our heavy, moist soil would fail to grow. Because of the south facing wall, and the specially made, open, well drained soil in the bed, it grows Mexican Salvias, cheiranthus, shrubby calceolaria, cistus, abutilon and numerous other Mediterranean plants.

This 'mediterranean bed' has been so successful, that we have now built another raised bed, L shaped, adjoining the original bed. It is 24 yards long 18 inches wide and 9-12 inches deep. Again the bed is filled with soil, peat and grit, and lots of grit and stones on the surface. These act as a mulch, the grit safeguards many alpines and dwarf shrubs in a bad winter, and in spring, summer and autumn helps to warm the soil. The concrete block sides absorb a tremendous amount of heat, whenever the sun shines, acting as heat stores, and slowly giving up the heat throughout the night.

Simple raised beds can be made without using cement and concrete blocks. Bricks can be laid dry on top of another on a levelled base, filling the spaces between with soil. A bed only two bricks high, i.e. six inches high, can make a tremendous difference to the growing of dwarf shrubs and alpines, especially when the bed is made up with plenty of grit.

Alternatively, a mound of prepared soil mixture could be retained by local stone or another suitable rocks. With a little ingenuity, many schemes can be adopted to make small or large raised beds. Long tree trunks or railway sleepers could also be used. Large tubs and pots can be utilised, but unless the bottom is removed so that they rest on the soil, they need too much watering in summer to be practical.

CHAPTER 10

Exotics

The use of south facing walls, banks and raised beds, for growing the more tender shrubs, was mentioned in the previous chapter. The term 'exotic plants,' is used in this chapter, to denote any plant not normally grown outside in this country, and covers plants from Australia, New Zealand, Chile, The Mediterranean countries and the Canary Isles.

On our very windswept nursery, sloping into the SW, and catching every conceivable wind, many of them off the sea, it is only possible to grow these exotic plants on south facing walls, and other well sheltered positions. So on the south wall of our house we are able grow Acacia dealbata and The Chilean Glory Vine. But for all the other fortunate people on west or south coasts, in more sheltered and sunny sites, these exotic plants can be grown in any favourable position.

It cannot be stressed too much, that all these mediterranean and other plants from warmer, sunnier lands, must be grown in well drained soil, if they are to survive the winter. Should the soil be close textured, and inclined to stick together after rain, plenty of coarse grit added before planting is essential. Also after planting a further surface dressing of grit around the stems will help considerably. Furthermore, if the soil is not light or sandy, gravel spread over the whole area in which you are growing mediterranean plants, will increase the soil temperature in spring and autumn.

Many other innovations can be used to grow exotic plants, where the ordinary soil would be unsuitable, such as is suggested in Chapter 9 on

Stones for drainage.   Ground level.

"Raised Beds". Another idea is to use the large 3 feet wide (or wider) concrete rings that are used in the making of a well, as a growing container. Stand the concrete ring on two or three inches of washed stones, and preferably near or against a south or other sunny wall. Fill it with a mixture of equal parts of good soil, peat and grit, and it is likely that some general fertiliser, such as Growmore will be needed, after a few years. It must be remembered that tubs, barrels, containers of any sort, will need a lot of watering in the summer, so make provision for this.

ABUTILON vitifolium, The *Chilean Mallow*, is the toughest of the abutilons. It has grey vine-shaped leaves and white or pale mauve flowers, like single hollyhocks, from June to July. It needs a very hot, dry situation. There are a lot of very colourful hybrid abutilons now available in a mixture of colours, one of these has a very striking gold variegated leaf, and orange flowers. These hybrids are best grown in pots, and put outside on a sunny, warm patio, or against south walls. They must be brought indoors at the first sign of frost.

ACACIA dealbata, The *Common Mimosa* will grow successfully outdoors, against a south wall, or in a sunny well drained site. It grows very fast, so will have to be pruned constantly, if grown against a wall. It rarely flowers outside, but will do so in an unheated glasshouse or porch, but do remember that if planted in soil (and not in a tub) it may push the roof off! It has beautiful green ferny foliage and golden flower puffs.

ACTINIDIA chinensis, The *Chinese Gooseberry* is a vigorous twining climber of noble aspect. Its very attractive leaves being 6-9 inches wide and its large, fragrant, white flowers changing to buff-yellow, appear in summer. The edible fruits are 1½-2 inches long, and are covered with brown hair. (Kiwi Fruit)

CALCEOLARIA integrifolia. This very beautiful Chilean shrub is a most dazzling spectacle from June to October (and often longer) covered entirely with large rounded clusters of golden pouch-shaped flowers. It grows into a rounded bush 3 feet high and the same in width. Good drainage and sunny position essential. Severe frost may kill it.

CALLISTEMON rigidus, The *Australian Bottle Brush* is a perfectly hardy evergreen by the coast. It grows to six feet with stiff, narrow, pointed leaves on arching branches. Nothing much to commend it, until it flowers, and then it is well worth its accommodation. It flowers June-July, and with its masses of large scarlet bottle brush flowers, presents a truly remarkable sight. To obtain the most spectacular show of flowers, put it in the warmest and sunniest spot in the garden.

CHEIRANTHUS, The *Perennial or Shrubby Wallflower* is probably the longest flowering dwarf shrub in our nurseries, flowering from May-December with deep, lilacy-mauve flowers. In mild winters, it continues into January. It grows into a rounded bush about 3 x 3 feet. There is also a yellow flowered cheiranthus, and a bicoloured one, but these grow much smaller, Good drainage and sunny position are essential.

70

CLIANTHUS puniceus, The *New Zealand Lobster Claw* is another remarkable evergreen with very pretty fern-like leaves on branches which fan outwards. It has scarlet flowers which resemble lobster claws, from April-July. It needs protection from frost, yet may survive a slight frost. Well drained soil, preferably sandy, and a sunny position are necessary. A mulch of grit around the base will help, and slug bait is essential in spring, when establishing young plants.

CRINODENDRON hookerianum, The *Chilean Lantern Bush* is indeed a true description for this gem of an evergreen. It flowers April-June, a dense mass of glowing crimson lanterns. In sheltered seaside locations it can grow to ten feet. Best in moist, loamy or peaty soils, but not water-logged. It will grow with some shade.

CYTISUS battandierei. This most unusual broom from Morocco, grows tall and lanky like a tree, and thus is best on the south wall of a house or tall building. Its large, clover-like leaves are covered with grey silky down. It needs a hot sunny position to bring out the cone shaped clusters of bright yellow flowers in July, which are deliciously scented of pineapple.

ECREMOCARPUS scaber, The *Chilean Glory Vine* is a tendril climber for trellis or netting, and needing a south wall. It has small, light green compound leaves and tubular orange flowers on the young shoots, from May to September. This is a very quick growing climber and is very showy, it also produces masses of seed.

EMBOTHRIUM lanceolatum, The *Chilean Fire Bush* is without doubt the most strikingly beautiful tree that can be grown in sheltered gardens. To visit Bodnant Gardens at the end of May, and see these embothriums 15-20 feet high, and covered with the brightest crimson scarlet tubular flowers, like those of honeysuckle, is an unforgettable sight. It is semi-evergreen and usually quite hardy by the coast. They require an acid soil, with plenty of humus, and a little shade.

EUCRYPHIA nymansay, is another beautiful small evergreen tree, with long narrow leaves, making rapid growth. It has spectacular, large white, fragrant flowers, somewhat like Christmas roses 2-2½ inches across, with a brush of stamens, in July and August. Best in lime free soil, with plenty of humus, and a little shade to the roots.

HIBISCUS syriacus, The *Tree Hollyhock,* is the hardy hibiscus, but does need a warm, sunny spot, and a good hot summer to induce flowering. They flower from July-October and their large trumpet shaped flowers, often 2 inches across, come in a variety of colours. It is a slow grower, but may reach 6-8 feet eventually.

LEPTOSPERMUM scoparium Nichollsii, The Crimson Manuka or New Zealand Tea Tree is an evergreen shrub related to the Myrtle. A very charming shrub, with its dainty growth of tiny, purple, thyme-like leaves on slender arching branches, and crimson blossoms in June. It must have full sun and a well drained site.

PHOENIX canariensis, The *Canary Island Date Palm* is the palm we meet all over the mediterranean as well as the Canary Isles, and other tropical places. It will not stand a great deal of frost, particularly when young. Therefore if an attempt is to be made to establish it in a very sheltered, and very warm and sunny seaside garden, it must continue to grow in a pot or container until it is about 1½-2 feet high. Even then, it would be wise to make a tent of fine plastic netting for it during the winter. Rich moist soils, excellent drainage and a very sunny spot are essential.

PITTOSPORUM tobira, The *Japanese Pittosporum* is a beautiful exotic shrub often seen in the mediterranean countries. It has dark green polished leaves and creamy white, orange scented flowers from April to July. A well drained soil and sunny position is essential. Very young plants may suffer from frost in their first and second winter. Likes to grow by a wall.

SALVIAS, The *Common Sage, Salvia officinalis* and the gold variegated, and the purple sage, I shall not be refering to here, but the more unusual Mexican Sages.

SALVIA fulgens grows 2-3 feet, with beautiful two inch long, velvety, red flowers from June to November. A really striking plant, but will not stand much frost.

S.grahamii is another long season flowering salvia with smaller, pink flowers which grows 2-3 feet. This variety is a little tougher than S.fulgens, as regards winter survival. *S.nurepia* with rosy red flowers from June to November, is the toughest of all the Mexican sages. *S.patens* has two inch long blue flowers throughout the summer, this too, like S.fulgens, is a rare, and most unusual and pretty salvia, but regrettably, the most tender of all. The safest way with all these Mexican salvias, is to grow them in large pots against a sunny wall, and to bring them indoors in winter. They are well worth the trouble.

TRACHYCARPUS fortunei, The *European Fan Palm*, or Windmill Palm is the hardiest of true palms. (Cordyline, mentioned in Chapter 5 although referred to as a palm, belongs to the genus Liliaceae, grows like a palm, but is not a true palm).

T.fortunei has enormous fan shaped leaves up to 2½ feet long, and 4 feet wide. Its trunk is densely covered with coarse hair-like fibres. This is a very slow growing palm, therefore it should be grown in a rich, moist, well drained soil, in a warm sheltered garden.

TREE HEATHS should be planted more often in seaside gardens, for they are a most rewarding group of plants, they all have very attractive, evergreen foliage, and grow from 3-6 feet tall. This group of heaths covers a flowering period from December to September. All flower abundantly, and the foliage of a feathery texture and many shades of green, is a very attractive feature.

ERICA arborea comes from the warmer parts of the Mediterranean coast, but is quite hardy in sheltered gardens on the coast. It has fragrant white flowers from March to May, and pale green foliage, it grows 4-6 feet. The variety *E.arborea alpina*, comes from the mountains of Spain, and is the hardiest of the arborea group, with white flowers and slight scent. *E.arborea Gold Tips* is identical to *E.arborea* except that the tips have a touch of gold in the spring. *E.arborea Pink Joy* has pink flowers and like all the other E.arboreas, grows 4-6 feet.

ERICA australis, The Spanish Heath comes from Spain and Portugal, with rosy red flowers from April to June, and grows to 6 feet. There is also a white flowered variety *E.australis Mr.Robert*, and a most striking variety with deep rosy red flowers. E.australis Riverslea, which is a magnificent sight when in flower.

ERICA codonodes, also called *E.Lustitanica*, The Portuguese Heath has the longest flowering period of all the tree heaths, from December to April. The flower buds are pink opening to white. It grows to six feet. This plant when fully grown, is a remarkable sight, with its soft pale green foliage, and flowers from ground level to the top, all through the worst winter weather. Because of this, it needs good staking; the weight of the snow could break the branches. In a very galey area, as at our nurseries, it was blown clean out of the ground, when it has grown to six feet tall, in eight years, and all because the tie to the stake had broken loose.

ERICA hibernica or *E.Mediterranea*. The Irish Heath, whilst not strictly a tree heath at all, has several very bushy varieties which grow 3-5 feet, which puts them in the same class as other tall growing tree heaths. This

73

Irish heath flowers from March to May and is lime tolerant.

E.mediterranea alba has very attractive, bright, light green foliage, and grows into a thick strong bush 3 x 3 feet with white flowers. *E.mediterranea superba* with foliage of a darker green, has flowers of rosy pink, with a honey scented aroma. It grows 4-5 feet tall, and just as wide, making a real sturdy bush. If grown as a hedge, it would be a truly remarkable and most unique sight, and it is strange that so few gardeners have discovered it.

ERICA terminalis or *E.stricta*, The Corsican Heath, comes from Corsica and Sardinia, and is definitely the hardiest of all the tree heaths. (E.hibernica comes second in hardiness) E.terminalis has rose coloured flowers from July to September and grows 3-4 feet high. This is another bushy heath that could be used as a hedge, and is tolerant of lime.

ERICA veitchii is a hybrid between E.arborea and E.codonodes, with honey scented white flowers from March to May. It grows to six feet. Like E.codonodes, this tree heath is a little tender, so should be given a sheltered sunny site.

Postscript November 1988

In the past ten years Britain has seen six bad winters, the severity of damage to trees and plants, being so unusual an occurence, that one wonders if the climate is undergoing a great change! Certainly in the 37 years that we have spent on our windswept nurseries near the sea, there has not been anything so bad as these six years, for damage to trees and shrubs.

Gardening by the sea gives one an opportunity to grow unusual and exotic plants, but in the event of extremes of frost or freezing winds, as mentioned above, it is obvious that these more tender plants will die, unless brought indoors or well protected. For plants left outdoors, this means they must be wrapped around with strips of foam plastic, or something of an open nature (not plastic sheeting) and finally well wrapped, including the top, with hessian or Rokolene or other windbreak netting. Do not use straw or hay inside, as mice will make nests in it and nibble the plant!

An adequate windbreak around your garden, whilst not proof against temperatures of 12-22 F (i.e. 10-20 F frost) nevertheless, by drastically reducing the speed of the wind, will save a lot of plants even with these temperatures.

As a final word, I can only say that all good gardeners must have patience, and a strong philosophical approach to life. This does not mean quietly accepting disasters without a murmur, but being prepared for the inevitable. In the period August to October, one must therefore take cuttings of all tender or doubtful plants that cannot be brought indoors. These cuttings must be kept in a glasshouse until the following April-June, when they can be potted on.

The author has now retired(?) to a very small nursery, some 33 miles north, but still near the sea, and still battling with the perennial problem of gales and salt winds! His "baptism of fire", came with the Jan 1990 hurricane, and five weeks of almost continuous gales. Even so, mediterranean plants are still becoming established in his gardens.